D1076261

X

INSIDE A SKYSCRAPER

BOBBI SEARLE

angus

This edition published in 2004
by Angus Books Ltd
12 Ravensbury Terrace
London SW18 4RL

ISBN 1-904594-55-7

© 2001 The Brown Reference Group plc

FOR BROWN PARTWORKS
Project editor: Roland Hall
Consultant: Dr. Derek Smith
Designer: Sarah Williams
Illustrators: Mike Fuller (main artwork), Mark Walker
Managing editor: Anne O'Daly
Picture researcher: Sean Hannaway

All rights reserved. Except for use in review, no part of this book may be reproduced, stored in a retrieval system, or transmitted in any form, or by any means, electronic, mechanical photocopying, recording, or otherwise, without prior permission of the publisher.

Production by Omnipress,
Eastbourne, UK
Printed and bound in Dubai

Contents

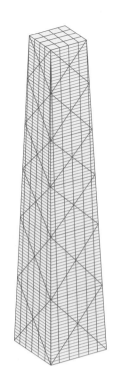

History of tall buildings

People have been constructing (building) tall buildings for centuries. Long before modern skyscrapers were developed, huge monuments were soaring into the sky. From ancient Egypt to modern Tokyo people have always adored tall buildings.

Pyramids are truly the forerunners of the modern skyscraper. The first pyramids were built in Egypt around 2500 B.C. The ancient Egyptians built these beautiful structures by piling huge stone blocks on top of each other. At 478 ft (146m) high the Great Pyramid in Giza was the tallest building in the world for thousands of years until cathedrals were built in Europe in the Middle Ages (approximately 850 A.D. to 1400 A.D.).

At the end of the 19th century there were new advances in technology. Steel was first used in buildings. It was stronger and lighter than previous materials. It was made by mixing the right amounts of iron and carbon. This was the start of a new age when building a long way up instead of out became possible. The other major advance was the elevator. It was invented in 1852 by Elisha Otis. Skyscrapers would not have been possible without the elevator because people did not think such tall buildings were worth having if they took a long time to climb.

In 1885 William Le Baron Jenney (with a team of builders) built the Home Insurance Building in Chicago. It was the world's first skyscraper. Le Baron Jenny used a steel frame

The Flat Iron Building. It was one of the first skyscrapers in New York and was built in 1902.

to construct the building. Shortly after this, people realized that using steel frames and reinforced concrete was an easy way to build huge buildings.

The first skyscraper ever built—the Home Insurance Building in Chicago.

Bigger and better

In 1931 the Empire State Building was built in New York City. It was the tallest skyscraper in the world for 42 years. It was 1,250 ft (381m) tall and it took 18 months to build. It is still one of the world's tallest buildings and it even survived an Air Force aeroplane crashing into it in 1945!

Techniques for making buildings bigger and bigger were developed. In 1974 the Sears Tower was completed in Chicago. It was 1,453 ft (443m) high and was the tallest skyscraper from 1973 to 1997. However, when the Petronas Towers were built in Kuala Lumpur, Malaysia, in 1998, a small matter of 30 ft (9m) meant they became the tallest skyscrapers in the world.

The Petronas Towers in Kuala Lumpur, Malaysia. Each tower has 88 stories.

Look inside a skyscraper

The way skyscrapers are built has changed as they have gotten bigger. People have found ways to make their skyscrapers higher and higher. One of the most popular ways to build high buildings is to construct a steel frame on a reinforced concrete foundation.

The Sears Tower in Chicago. You can see over 40 miles (60km) from the 103rd floor.

FACT FILE

○ Skyscrapers are mostly built in the same way. Reinforced concrete foundations support steel-framed structures.

○ Some skyscrapers have concrete structures.

○ Concrete or steel-girder floors are added as the building is put together.

○ Over 1.5 million people visit the Sears Tower in Chicago (pictured below) every year to ride up and look from the top. Have a look at the web site: http://www.sears-tower.com

Helipad
Some skyscrapers have helipads on top for helicopters to land on.

Services
Service features like water supply and electricity supply, pipes, and cables are stored on special service floors and in the spaces between other floors.

Steel frame
The long pieces of metal (girders) are bolted together for strength.

Elevator shafts
They are usually found deep in the building, where daylight is not needed.

Reinforced concrete foundations
They are built deep into the ground.

Revolving doors
Skyscrapers often have revolving doors. They minimize the effects of high winds.

Laying foundations

There are problems with building tall buildings that you do not get with smaller ones. This is how skyscrapers are constructed.

The site is surveyed

A skyscraper is only as solid as the ground it is built on, so a survey of the ground is always carried out before the foundations are laid. It is important to find out the type of soil and rock in the ground so that the enormous building does not subside (sink into the ground) after it has been built.

Clearing the site

Any existing buildings on the construction site for the skyscraper need to be demolished and cleared away. Large cranes, diggers and drills are used to break up and carry away the debris. Surveyors can then measure where the foundations for the new building will go (setting out the site) and work can begin.

Construction of the foundations

So that the building does not move around after it has been built, foundations are laid deep in the ground. This provides a solid base to work on when construction of the rest of the building begins.

The building process

Once the foundations have been laid, the skyscraper starts to take shape. A skyscraper's large frame, which is put together piece by piece, is like the skeleton of the building. Huge columns are attached to the foundations, and horizontal beams are fastened to the columns to keep the structure strong.

This site is about to have a skyscraper built on it. The ground has been levelled and the holes for the foundations have been started.

Moving on up

As the skyscraper gets higher, cranes are needed to lift heavy materials and equipment like steel beams and concrete to different levels in the building. Cranes are bolted to the outside of the steel frame once it gets above ground level so that the cranes will be extra secure.

Prefabricated components

Because skyscrapers are such huge buildings, many of the materials are made before the construction starts (prefabricated) and are then transported to the site piece by piece when they are needed. The steel beams and concrete floors are prefabricated.

CONCRETE CORE

1. Many skyscrapers are built with a central concrete core. The core is made from concrete that is reinforced with steel wires or bars.

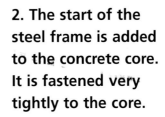

2. The start of the steel frame is added to the concrete core. It is fastened very tightly to the core.

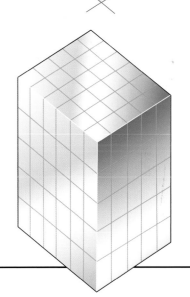

3. More steel is added to the frame that surrounds the concrete core. The steel forms a "cage" that reinforces (makes it stronger) and supports the building.

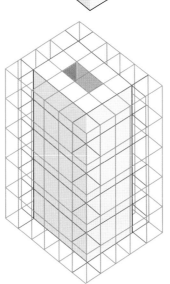

4. When all the steel has been bolted or welded together, the outer layer of the building is added. This building's outer layer is made of glass. Other skyscrapers have aluminium or concrete on the outside.

Building higher

When the basic frame of the building has been completed, the floors, outer walls and other parts of the building are put in.

Construction of the floors

The floors of skyscrapers need to be very strong but light, so they are made from strips of corrugated steel, which are laid side by side on the steel beams of the frame. Sometimes the floors are covered in a layer of concrete for extra strength. In some skyscrapers the floors are made of concrete only. The concrete is usually mixed somewhere else and delivered to the building site.

The outer walls

The outer wall (sheeting) of a skyscraper is very important because it keeps the building dry and quiet. Sheeting must be as light as possible because the steel frame has to support the outer walls. Too much weight can cause failures. Some skyscrapers are covered in glass, coloured stone or aluminium

Above: Tons of concrete are poured over steel bars to make reinforced concrete. When it hardens, it will be very strong.

to make them look extra special. On some skyscrapers the sheeting helps hold the building up; it takes some of the load.

Services and lifts

Each floor of a skyscraper needs to have access to all of the essential services, such as heating, electricity and running water. This ensures offices, toilets and kitchens can be used. Tall buildings also need to provide another form of access than stairs, for example, lifts. All these services are often contained in the middle of the building, called the central core.

FACT FILE

○ When the Hong Kong and Shanghai Bank was built in Hong Kong, the foundations were dug by people, not machines. It was cheaper, more efficient and there was very little space in the building site.

○ Concrete and other components (parts of a building) are sometimes made away from building sites and delivered. This is called prefabricating.

○ When you next see a building site, try to guess where the building will be placed. Judge this by the holes in the ground. If the building is already being built, look at the way it is being put together. How tall do you think it will be when it is finished?

Construction of rooms

The rooms in a skyscraper are built very simply. The large floors are divided into rooms by metal frames. They are called studs. Sheets of dividing material, for example, plasterboard, are attached with screws over this frame to make the walls. Rooms in skyscrapers are specially designed to make it easy to change them around, for example, when somebody new moves into an office.

The finishing process

Once everything is in place, the decoration inside the building needs to be done. The engineers carry out a final check of all the machinery and equipment before they leave. Car parks or gardens will also need to be finished. Most skyscrapers have a special opening ceremony when a famous person will officially open the building.

TEST OF STRENGTH

1 Use a large sheet of paper and the templates shown below to make the shapes. Glue the ends together. They will be your beams.

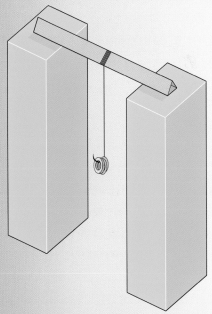

2 Hang string around a beam and add a wire hook to the string. Place a beam between two solid surfaces. Test the strength of your beams by adding washers until the beams collapse. Which beam is the strongest? Does it make a difference if the ends are glued together?

Materials

Skyscrapers are made from modern materials, some of which were only developed in the last 200 years.

Concrete is strong and so is very good for construction, but it is not always ideal for skyscrapers because it is very heavy. Very tall skyscrapers need extra strength, so they are built using strong steel frames instead. Some smaller skyscrapers can be built entirely from concrete, but most of the biggest skyscrapers built use a mixture of steel and reinforced concrete frames.

Concrete is a mixture of small stones, water and cement. When it dries or sets, it becomes very strong. Cement can break when it is stretched, so it is often reinforced. This involves giving it extra strength by burying steel bars in it. Concrete is a paste before it

Steel is made from iron and carbon. They are mixed together when they are both very hot.

sets, so you can preform it into many different shapes.

Steel is very strong, but it can bend and even break under the weight of huge skyscrapers. To stop this from happening,

REINFORCED CONCRETE

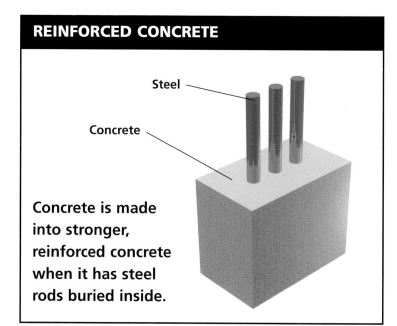

Steel

Concrete

Concrete is made into stronger, reinforced concrete when it has steel rods buried inside.

the beams and columns in the frames of skyscrapers are formed into special shapes.

Steel for strength

Steel is a mixture of iron and carbon, which makes it very strong. Ordinary steel rusts, so it is usually given a protective coating of paint, plastic, or a non-rusting metal such as zinc.

Sections in the steel frame of skyscrapers are bolted together or melted together (welded) using hot molten metal for extra strength. When many small joins are needed, rivets are often used. Rivets are special pins that attach two sheets together. They are cheaper and quicker to use than nuts and bolts. Imagine having to tighten over one billion nuts and bolts on a skyscraper!

Glass is manufactured by mixing sand, limestone and soda ash and then heating it up.

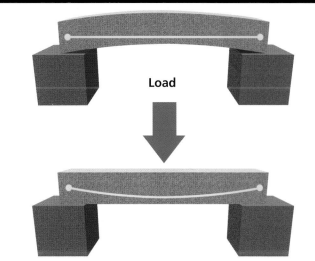

PRE-STRESSED CONCRETE

Load

A pre-stressed concrete beam is bent upward when there is no load on it because the wires are in tension. When there is a load on it, the concrete beam bendsandthe wire inside it is stretched tighter. Prestressed concrete stays strong when under pressure.

At your service

The air conditioning, lifts, water and electricity in a building have to go somewhere. They are all usually stored in the middle of the skyscraper.

There are many reasons why lifts are usually in the middle of a skyscraper. In the event of any emergency the lifts and any rescue stairs must be well positioned and protected in the middle of the building, usually in the central concrete core if there is one. Some buildings have lifts on the outside. This can be nice for the passengers and can create extra space inside the building, but it can be expensive (and not good for people who are scared of heights!).

The idea of the lift has been around for a long time. However, until the first "safety" lift was invented in 1852 by Elisha Otis, people did not trust them. Most lifts are simply a box—the lift car—on the end of a piece of string—a steel cable. The string is thrown over a pulley and then tied to a counterweight. A motor pulls the box up and lets it down with help from the counterweight. The motor that is connected to the pulley does not have a lot of work to do. The reason we can be confident in an lift is because of the safety brake. It activates if there is a failure of any kind. The safety brake clamps the lift in its shaft and prevents it from falling.

This lift is situated inside a building. You can see the doors that open when the lift reaches different floors of the building.

The lift that uses this deep shaft is round. You can see the guide rails for the lift car.

Servicing a skyscraper

Every skyscraper needs access to water, electricity, and heat. Piping (for water) and ducting (for electricity and air conditioning) usually run through the middle of the building. This way, electricity and water can be efficiently piped to each floor.

To help reduce power usage and to make the building more efficient, most water systems have help from gravity. When a large water tank is placed on the roof, water can flow naturally down the pipes into the rooms of the skyscraper. Water is pumped up from the ground when the tank is low on water.

Most modern skyscrapers also have air conditioning. It cools people down when they are hot and it circulates air without having to open lots of windows. It also heats people up when they are cold.

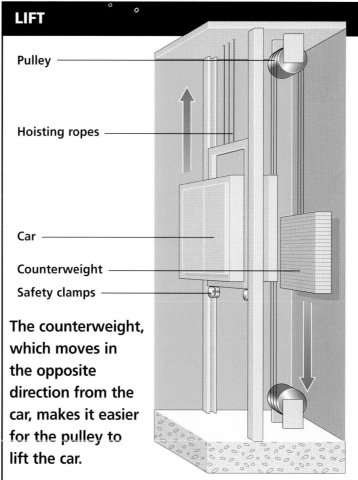

LIFT

Pulley

Hoisting ropes

Car

Counterweight

Safety clamps

The counterweight, which moves in the opposite direction from the car, makes it easier for the pulley to lift the car.

Back to the drawing board

Before any of the construction of a skyscraper can take place, the building is planned and designed for months or even years. Some skyscrapers have been planned but never been built. Sometimes the developers run out of money, or the city decides it does not want another big building.

The long planning process begins with the architect who will design the building. The architect makes sketches after visiting the site for the building. He or she has to make sure that it will blend in with the surrounding area. Tall buildings can cast huge shadows, so the height and shape of the design are very important, even at this early stage. When the sketches are done, the architect works with structural engineers to design the foundations. The structural engineers can help tell the architect if his or her design will work properly or not.

Architects' plans and drawings are not always sketched on paper. Many modern architects use computer-aided design (CAD) systems to help with their designs. They allow the architect and engineers to view a virtual-reality (built using a computer) design from all angles and get a feel for what the finished building will look like and how it will affect the surrounding area.

FACT FILE

○ Architects draw hundreds or even thousands of drawings of a building to get a good idea of how it will look and how it will affect its environment.

○ Using computers, architects can construct "virtual" buildings and see what it would be like to walk around inside them.

○ Have a look for building "sites" on the Internet. You may even find virtual reality walkthroughs. You could try http://www.greatbuildings.com

This picture is an architects' drawing of what the landscape will look like when the building has been constructed.

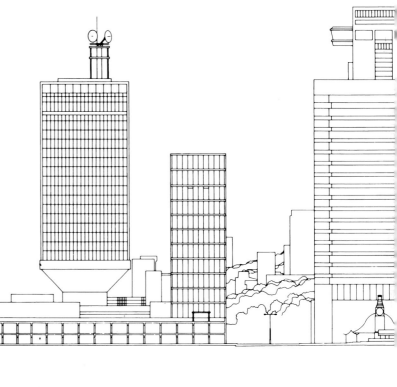

Tough enough

It is very important to know that a building will be strong enough once it is built. It must withstand the weight—or load—of all the heavy building materials and equipment, as well as the people working or visiting the skyscraper. The designers use small models to test the strength of the proposed building.

Architects and engineers also test any new materials for the planned skyscraper before it is built. They check that the materials are strong enough and are able to resist extreme weather conditions. If the building is to be built in an area where there are a lot of earthquakes or high winds, the planners must make sure that the building will be strong enough to withstand any extreme forces. In several countries such as Hong Kong (shown below), architects must make their buildings resistant to typhoons (strong winds in the Pacific Ocean) that occur in the area.

This house is being tested to see how well it would survive if it was affected by an earthquake.

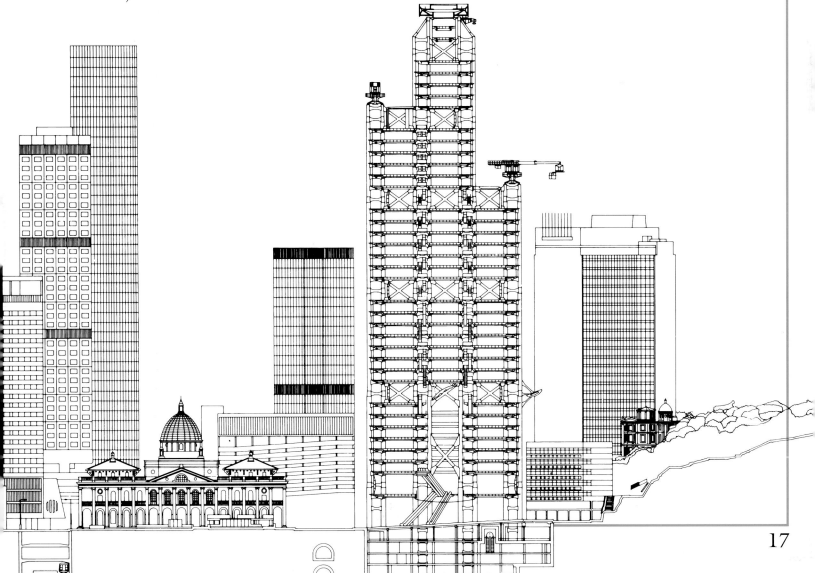

17

A place for people

Most modern office buildings are owned by one large company and leased (rented) to people inside (tenants).

Any office partitions put up in a skyscraper are usually temporary. The owner of the building can change each office space very quickly to suit the needs of any new tenants.

Some things stay the same in offices. Before modern fluorescent strip lighting, designers had to think very carefully about where and how close to the windows their offices were. It was difficult to properly light up large areas of office space. Nowadays, with strip lighting, we can all have plenty of light to work in wherever we are in a building. Lights like these do not need to be changed when new people move into an office.

Above: These window cleaners are standing on a platform that has been specially designed to allow people to work on the building.

Windows are no use if they are dirty. So how do you clean a window that is 40 stories up? Most skyscrapers use a "cradle." It is like an external lift in which two or more window cleaners can travel up and down the outside of the building cleaning the glass. Sometimes—if the shape of a building has lots of unusual corners and angles—people abseil (descend on ropes) down the side and clean the windows this way. The Petronas Towers have cranelike arms that lower window cleaners down the buildings. Some buildings have machines that automatically clean the windows. They are set into the steel supports and are controlled by computers.

Living and working space

Skyscrapers are not always just for offices. Lots of them are used for work, but many of them serve a different purpose. Thousands of people all over the world live in apartments inside skyscrapers.

Many skyscrapers have become almost self-sufficient mini towns. They have everything that you would find in a normal town or even city: shops, restaurants, and leisure and sports centres. The fashion for the future of skyscrapers could be for places like these, where people can work, live and play without having to leave the building.

Most skyscapers are built to house offices like this one in Tokyo. Some skyscrapers have stores and leisure centres in them as well.

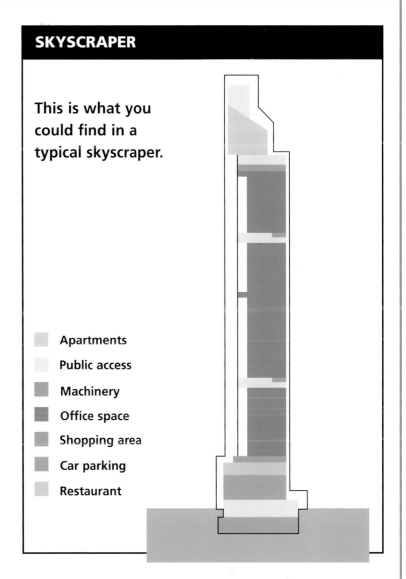

SKYSCRAPER

This is what you could find in a typical skyscraper.

- Apartments
- Public access
- Machinery
- Office space
- Shopping area
- Car parking
- Restaurant

Windy city

Testing models of skyscrapers in wind tunnels is very important because in strong winds the top of a tall building can sway (move from side to side) up to a yard (1m).

To minimize the sway of skyscrapers, some buildings are braced. This means that they are strengthened with diagonal steel sections, or that they are built with a strong central reinforced concrete core. The core helps prevent the building from moving around in strong winds.

Some buildings—especially those in earthquake-prone areas or places where there are lots of high winds—have something called a "tuned mass damper" inside them. It is a device that prevents the building from swaying too much. There is a huge weight in

Wind tunnel studies are carried out on a model of a building. The tunnel can blow out winds equivalent to over 60 miles per hour (100km/h).

the top of the building. Computers measure the amount of sway and then move the weight (damper) in the opposite direction to counterbalance the building.

Wind power

If you have ever walked past a skyscraper, you probably noticed that it was very windy. This is a common problem with such tall

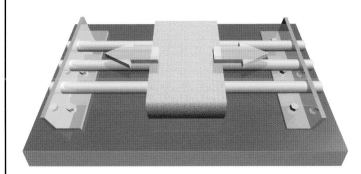

If a building sways from side to side, the tuned mass damper—stored at the top—moves a heavy weight across to counteract the force and stabilize the building.

A model of Hong Kong. This model was built so that the architects could see how wind would affect their new building.

buildings. Skyscrapers can funnel winds between them, so constructing two tall buildings next to each other can be a bad idea because the force of the wind between them can be immense. People do like to build pairs of tall buildings at the same time—the Petronas Towers in Kuala Lumpur, Malaysia

are tapering twin towers built close to one another and connected by a sky bridge.

A very important part of skyscraper design is the entrance because of the problem of high winds. A good design can shield people entering or leaving the building from the force of the wind so that they do not get blown over. Revolving doors are also very good at preventing energy being lost from the building every time the door is opened.

The old New York skyline with the twin towers- which were the 2 tallest buildings before the September 11th attack.

Tall stories

Not all tall buildings are skyscrapers. In fact, the tallest human-made structure is not a skyscraper.

There are many other structures that need to be tall because of the job that they do. Imagine an oil rig or a lighthouse built just a few yards above the level of the water or a sports stadium no bigger than your school hall. Structures sited at sea or places that need to hold a lot of people have to be built tall.

The Eiffel Tower was built in Paris in 1889 for an exhibition. Gustav Eiffel built it to show that tall structures could be made out of steel. After the exhibition the people of Paris decided that they liked the tower, so they kept it. From 1889 to 1931 it was the tallest structure in the world.

Above: The tallest human-made structure in the world: the CN Tower in Toronto, Canada.

Left: The Eiffel Tower took two years to build between 1887 and 1889.

The world's first lighthouse was built near Alexandria in Egypt in 270 B.C. It was 400 ft (122m) high. The light to guide ships was produced by an open fire, which had to be kept burning all through the night.

Tallest of the tall

Huge radio and television antennas are very tall structures that are sometimes supported by steel guy wires. The CN Tower in Toronto, Canada, is a 1,820-ft (555-m) television transmission antenna. It is the tallest building in the world, but it is not a skyscraper because it does not house offices or apartments.

Modern windmills called wind turbines are often used to produce electricity. They are large windmills on huge towers and have two or three blades. They convert the power of the wind into electricity using a generator. The head (top) of the windmill can also move to make sure that the blades are always facing the wind. These very tall structures all need to be extremely strong to withstand the force of the wind so that they do not fall over.

Above: Wind farms are normally built in the windiest places, usually on the tops of hills. This wind farm is in Spain.

SIZE MATTERS

This diagram shows the relative sizes of some of the most important buildings throughout history. The buildings are (from left to right):
The Great Pyramid (Egypt),
The Empire State Building (U.S.),
The Petronas Towers (Malaysia),
The Eiffel Tower (France), and
The CN Tower (Canada).

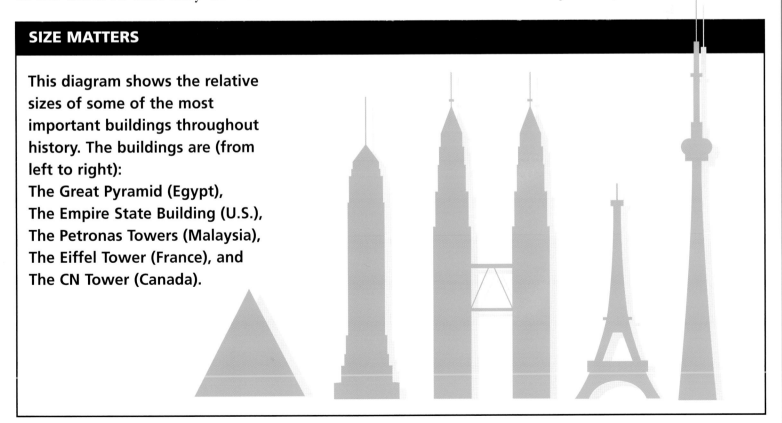

Different designs—many ways to build a skyscraper

Not all skyscrapers are built in the same way. The way skyscrapers are built has changed as people have built them higher and higher.

Architects and engineers often choose to combine different skyscraper designs to produce a different building for each different location. In a country prone to earthquakes or hurricanes a structure would have to mix traditional skyscraper designs with high-tech designs to withstand the earth tremors (earthquakes) or very high winds. Some skyscrapers need to be stronger than others.

BUILD A SKYSCRAPER

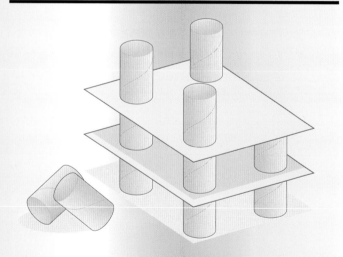

1 You will need some old paper tubes and some cardboard.

2 Construct your own tall building as shown in the diagram above. How high can you build your skyscraper? Very tall buildings become less stable the taller they get.

This building has been stripped back to show the concrete core that steadies the steel frame. The lifts are visible inside.

Rigid-frame structure—The frame is made up of columns and connecting beams, with each section of the design carrying the load of the structure. The first skyscrapers were built this way, with the walls carrying some of the load of the building. An advance on this was the stronger braced-frame structure.

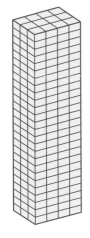

Braced-frame structure— This is like a rigid frame design, but it has bracing added to improve stability and reduce the side-to-side sway of the building. Skyscrapers built this way can be higher and stronger than rigid-frame structure skyscrapers. They are very stable so are good to build in earthquake-threatened and very windy areas.

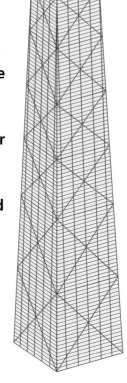

Concrete core construction— This design includes a central core made of concrete, suspended columns, and strong beams and floor supports. The walls do not bear any load, and the floors are suspended from the central column. This type of skyscraper is strong enough for buildings about 40 stories high in non-earthquake countries.

Framed concrete core— This design is similar to the concrete core, but the building has an external steel or concrete frame as well as the concrete core. The two frames (internal concrete and external steel) act together to maximize resistance to wind. An advance on this design was the concrete tube-in-tube construction, which allowed skyscrapers to be even stronger and taller.

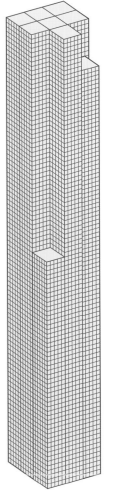

Steel-framed tube and bundled tube—These structures are very strong and allow skyscrapers to be more than 100 stories high. A steel-framed tube structure is made of steel beams, which are connected to each other. All the internal parts of the building are attached to the steel beams. In a bundled-tube building the steel tubes are joined together in groups to make an even stronger and taller structure.

Disaster!

Earthquakes are frightening events at the best of times but imagine being trapped in a skyscraper when one was happening!

For any building to survive an earthquake the important thing is for the materials used to be able to bend—rather than break—with the vibrations and tremors. Engineers have worked hard to prevent tall skyscrapers moving and shaking during an earthquake by designing special rubber bearings for the foundations. They help the building absorb (soak up) the effects of the earth's movement and remain upright.

In the event of an emergency evacuation from a skyscraper there are always many ways out of the building. There are also rescue stairs within a skyscraper—usually in the middle of the building where it is safest—so that people can escape by foot. Lifts are not normally used for evacuation because of the risk of mechanical failure.

FACT FILE

⊙ *The Towering Inferno* is a famous scary movie about a fire in a skyscraper.

⊙ There are about half a million earthquakes every year around the world. Most of them are small and do not affect anybody.

⊙ One of the worst earthquakes was in 1976, in China. Around 750,000 people were killed.

⊙ To hear what an earthquake sounds like on the Internet, try:
http://quake.wr.usgs.gov/more/listen

Safe in the air

It is not just people inside a skyscraper who may be in danger. It is very important that pilots flying aeroplanes near the tops of skyscrapers can see them clearly at all times so that they do not crash into them. Very tall buildings have flashing lights at the top so that they are always clearly visible during the day and night.

Fire breaking out in a skyscraper is a horrible thought. To improve fire resistance, most skyscrapers are now equipped with automatic sprinkler systems. They are activated by electronic sensors on every floor when smoke is detected. A fire alarm is sounded automatically. Some modern skyscrapers also have pressurization systems. They increase the air pressure in the escape routes. That makes it harder for smoke to escape from any room that may be on fire. The steel frame of a skyscraper does not burn easily. It can bend in the heat, so to prevent that, the steel is coated with insulation.

Whole streets were destroyed in this earthquake in Kobe, Japan, in 1996.

Right: This building collapsed because it was not strong enough to survive an earthquake. It happened in Los Angeles in 1984.

The future

Ever since the first skyscrapers people have wanted to build even bigger and higher buildings. As the 21st century goes on, some countries are running out of space to house all the people who live in them.

Some countries, particularly in Asia, will need to build more and more skyscrapers as their populations increase rapidly. Sky City 1000 is a project designed by Japanese architects to build a skyscraper 3,000 ft (1,000m) high—that is, twice as high as the current tallest building. Rather than different floors or stories, it would have mini towns, which would contain houses, offices, shops and even parks and gardens. The Millennium Tower is another Japanese project to build a 2,438-ft (800-m) high steel-framed skyscraper in the middle of an artificial lagoon.

Advanced building

The race is on to improve the technology within skyscrapers to make them as efficient and cost effective as possible. Intelligent buildings that are able to monitor (check) themselves are starting to appear. For example, if you became too hot, the building would tell its computers to control the airflow inside and cool it down. If it was too cold, then the same airflow can be used for heating. The buildings can even control large mirrors that reflect natural daylight into darker parts of the skyscraper that are not close to windows.

The Millennium Tower. This is a made-up photograph of a model of the tower. The tower's foundations will be in water.

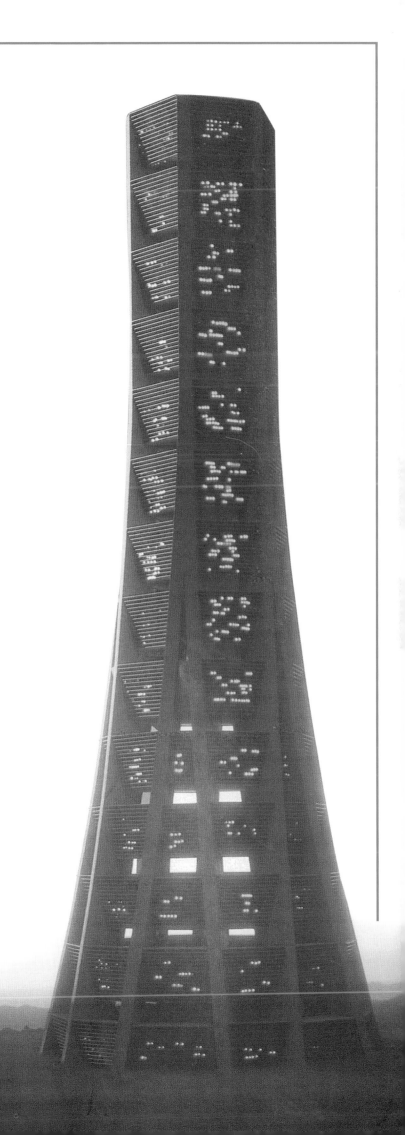

FACT FILE

◯ Fewer skyscrapers were built during the 1990s than in the previous 40 years.

◯ "Green" skyscrapers are being built. No. 4 Times Square in New York is a building that will be made using fewer materials than traditional buildings, will be much cheaper to run and will recycle its own waste.

◯ There are some amazing buildings planned in the future. Have a look at them on the Internet. Try http://www-eleves.int-evry.fr/~durand_f/ar00.htm

Reaching for the sky

X-Seed 4000 is a project designed by the Taisei Corporation, a Japanese company, to build a 12,000-ft (4,000-m) skyscraper that will "float" in the Bay of Tokyo in Japan. X-Seed will be unlike traditional skyscrapers in many ways—it will be shaped like a volcano, it will be powered by solar energy (from the sun), and it will be able to react to the weather conditions outside to keep the light, temperature and air pressure the same inside. Construction of X-Seed 4000 should be started by 2030, and it will house one million people when it is finished.

Planning pyramids

The religious leader Maharishi Mahesh Yogi is planning to have two huge buildings built for him and his followers. The larger of the two will be 2,222 ft (677m) high. It will be built in India. Both of the buildings will be pyramid-shaped, just like ancient Egyptian pyramids—ancestors of today's skyscrapers.

Sky City 1000 is a very futuristic-looking building. People will be able to live all of their lives in it.

Glossary

AUTOMATIC FIRE-SPRINKLER SYSTEM—a computer-controlled emergency system of fire extinguishers that operates automatically with a sudden rise in temperature.

BEARINGS—a part of a machine or structure that reduces friction or sideways forces between two surfaces (the ground and the foundations of a skyscraper, for example).

BRACE—to stiffen or strengthen a structure by connecting two or more of its sections together diagonally.

COUNTERWEIGHT—a weight that is attached to one part of a machine or structure to balance the weight of a load elsewhere.

CORRUGATED—shaped or formed in grooves or wavy lines.

HEAT EXCHANGER—a device in which heat is taken from a hot liquid or gas—the coolant—in order to warm a cool one. The pipes containing the hot fluid usually pass through the cool fluid.

INTELLIGENT BUILDING—a computer-controlled building that is able to respond to changes in its environment internally and externally to control temperature, lighting, and air-pressure levels.

MODULE—a separate unit, section or compartment that forms part of a structure.

PREFABRICATE—to build standardized parts—walls, roof and floors—for a structure away from the building site for assembling later.

PRESSURIZATION SYSTEM—a device that maintains normal atmospheric pressure in a building and responds to fire by increasing the air pressure in hallways and stairs to reduce the risk of it spreading.

SERVICES—essential facilities in a structure such as toilets, heating and lighting as well as lifts, stairs and electrical cabling.

SUBSIDE—the process of a structure's foundations settling down or sinking to a lower level after it has been built.

TUNED MASS DAMPER—a device attached to a structure that minimizes sway during an earthquake by absorbing the vibrations and preventing any sudden movements.

VIRTUAL REALITY—a computer-operated simulator that creates an imaginary world or three-dimensional object that you are able to manipulate.

FURTHER INFORMATION

Books to read:
Skyscrapers by Judith Dupré; Black Dog & Leventhal, New York, NY, 1996.
Skyscrapers: A Fold-Out Book by Nicholas Harris; Rand McNally, Skokie, Il, 1995.

Or you could try visiting a skyscraper in a big city in your area.

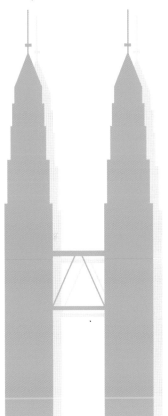

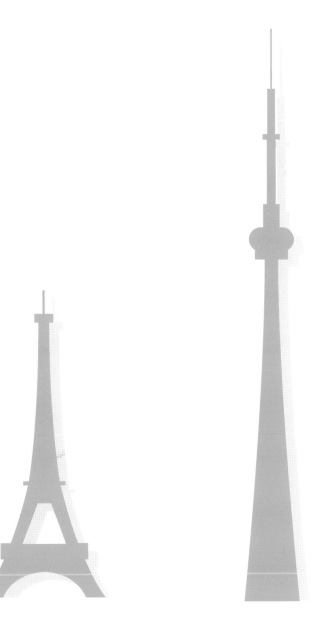

Index

PICTURE CREDITS Cesar Pelli & Associates Inc. 5r J. Apicella **Corbis** 5tl, 6b and cover Roger Ressmeyer, 12t Scott Smith, 17tr Roger Ressmeyer, 18t and cover Kevin Fleming, 22bl, 26bl Michael Yamashita, 27c Joseph Sohm **Sylvia Cordaiy Photo Library** 24br Geoffrey Taunton **Ecoscene Photo Library** 23tr Erik Schaffer **Foster & Partners** 10t John Nye, 16 & 17b, 21tr, 28l Richard Davies **Hulton Getty** 4tr **Image Bank** 15t Pete Turner, 19b Kaz Mori **David Noble Photography** 21b, 22r, 30 & 31b **Otis** 14l **Pilkington** 13b **Science Photo Library** 20t Takenaka Corporation 29r **Travel Ink Photo & Feature Library** 8 & 9b and cover Derek Allan (t-top b-bottom r-right l-left c-center)